T0011994

CHAPTER
ONE

Those first cuts of the avocado, calculating whether it is too soon or, God forbid, too late. There is something mystical about the unknown ripeness you think you can feel as you give it a gentle squeeze. Cradling your prize while wielding a sharp knife to remove the stone becomes a test of not only nerves but dexterity and commitment. The magical unsheathing of the soft bright green flesh from its brown nut-like skin, peeling it back with a delicacy saved only for a newborn baby.

With a history that makes it older than the invention of the wheel, the avocado has been touted as many things: an aphrodisiac, superfood and a symbol of wealth, to name but a few.

So throw out your preconceptions of "it's all just guac" and dive into this fruitful guide of all things green.

INTRODUCTION

Long before we were scouring the supermarket aisles secretly squeezing each green goddess for the perfect specimen to smash, crush, mush and blend our way to brunch perfection, the avocado had seeded itself into the lives of man and beast alike.

But what makes the avocado *so* special? So popular that it became the symbol of every millennial's failure to climb the housing ladder? And why are we willing to pay a high price for it to be artfully placed on piece of sourdough toast along with our chai lattes?

For many, the perfectly ripe avocado holds a god-like status. Forget stealing three of the golden apples of the Hesperides, finding one is akin to a modern-day task Hercules might have faced if he lived among us mortals. It has become a 21st-century ritual.

THE LITTLE BOOK OF

AVOCADO

Published in 2024 by OH!
An Imprint of Welbeck Non-Fiction Limited,
part of Welbeck Publishing Group.
Offices in: London – 20 Mortimer Street, London W1T 3JW
and Sydney – Level 17, 207 Kent St, Sydney NSW 2000 Australia
www.welbeckpublishing.com

Compilation text © Welbeck Non-Fiction Limited 2023
Design © Welbeck Non-Fiction Limited 2023

Disclaimer:
This book is intended for general informational purposes only and should not be relied upon as recommending or promoting any specific practice, diet or method of treatment. It is not intended to diagnose, advise, treat or prevent any illness or condition and is not a substitute for advice from a professional practitioner of the subject matter contained in this book. You should not use the information in this book as a substitute for medication, nutritional, diet, spiritual or other treatment that is prescribed by your practitioner. The publisher makes no representations or warranties with respect to the accuracy, completeness or currency of the contents of this work, and specifically disclaim, without limitation, any implied warranties of merchantability or fitness for a particular purpose and any injury, illness, damage, death, liability or loss incurred, directly or indirectly from the use or application of any of the contents of this book. Furthermore, the publisher is not affiliated with and does not sponsor or endorse any uses of or beliefs about in any way referred in this book.

ISBN 978-1-80069-033-2

Compiled and by: Caroline Fleming
Editorial: Victoria Denne
Project manager: Russell Porter
Design: Tony Seddon
Production: Jess Brisley

A CIP catalogue record for this book is available from the British Library

Printed in China

10 9 8 7 6 5 4 3 2 1

Illustrations: Freepik.com

THE LITTLE BOOK OF
AVOCADO

THE PERFECT SUPERFOOD

CONTENTS

You had me at "avocado"

Sit back and be bathed in the warm green glow of everything avocado...

Although considered a fruit, the avocado is in fact a large berry containing a single large seed (or pit) found growing on a tree of the same name.

The genus name for
the avocado tree is
Persea americana, which
comes from the Greek
name, *persea*, for an
Egyptian tree.

The avocado tree makes up just one of the 2,850 species of the flowering plant family *Lauraceae*, the laurels.

Avocados and cinnamon are both species of laurels.

The avocado is the lone edible fruit in the laurel family.

Avocado trees
grow both male and
female flowers.

Avocado trees do not self-pollinate; they need another avocado tree close by to bear fruit.

An avocado tree can live
for 400 years and grow
to the height of 70 feet
(21 metres).

The roots of an avocado tree are strong and aggressive. So much so that they can break concrete pavements as they grow.

One avocado tree
can produce between
200 and 500 avocados
per year.

Avocados are toxic to horses, as are their skins to cats and dogs.

Stealing avocados in
California, USA, is a
felony punishable by up
to 3 years in state prison.

There are well over 500 varieties of avocado, which vary in texture, size, shape and maturity rate. **Here are our picks!**

Bacon

A Californian original, the
Bacon avocado is medium in
size with a uniform oval shape
and green colour.

Choquette

A large oval avocado from
Southern Florida, the
Choquette is the very large
fruit with a watery flesh and
a mild taste.

Ettinger

A particular favourite in Israel, this medium-sized avocado is known for its shiny, delicate skin.

Fuerte

Mainly found in Mexico and Central America, the Fuerte avocado is considered to be the "original" avocado. Its elongated form and ease to peel made it the most popular avocado in America for many years.

Gwen

Developed in California, the Gwen has a similar taste to the Hass, with dark green skin and a nutty flavour.

Hass

The celebrity of the avocado world, the Hass avocado is distinctive for skin that turns from green to purplish black when ripe.

Lula

Originating in Southern Florida, this cold-resistant avocado has a glossy green skin.

Maluma

Discovered in South Africa in the 1990s, the Maluma, sometimes called the Maluma Hass due to its similarity in appearance to the well-known avocado, is a large fruit with a black, purple skin when ripe.

Pinkerton

Characterized by light green, creamy flesh and small seed in an elongated body, the Pinkerton has a thick, rough skin that can be easily peeled.

Zutano

A medium fruit with a thin skin, the Zutano belongs to the Mexican family of avocados and is known for its mild flavour.

While considered vegan, it has been argued that as a result of the migratory beekeeping needed to pollinate the fruit, avocados could be considered off-limits to strict vegans.

The "cocktail" avocado first hit the shelves of Marks & Spencer's in 2017. Between 5 cm and 8 cm, they are named not just for their small size, but because they can be eaten whole, as they have no seed!

The product of an unpollinated blossom, seedless avocados are not something new. In fact, they regularly appear on avocado trees and are known as "cukes" to those in the know.

The "Avozilla" is a cross between two types of avocado, the West Indian and the Guatemalan varieties, and is five times the size of an average avocado.

Zilla Eggs, or egg-vocados as they are nicknamed, started appearing in 2017, named so because they are the size of an egg, or a third of the size of an average avocado.

Avocados? Or Avocadoes?

According to the US Merriam-Webster dictionary, either is correct.

The Cambridge Dictionary disagrees, however, arguing "avocados" is the proper spelling of the plural.

Potato, potahto, tomato, tomahto! Let's just eat some guac!

The Netherlands is the world's second-largest importer of avocados, but 79% of the import is re-exported to Europe.

The Mexican state of Michoacán produces 8 out of 10 Mexican avocados and 5 out of 10 avocados produced globally.

California
produces 90% of the
US avocado crop.

The first mega fans
of the avocados were
the megafauna of the
Cenozoic era, 66 million
years ago.

The Aztecs were the first to start cultivating the avocado, but they had a different name for it, *āhuacatl*, which also means testicles.

Given the fact that they grow in pairs, are a similar shape and have a rough texture – plus they're considered to be an aphrodisiac – we think they can be forgiven.

Each year, 11 billion lbs
(4 billion kg) of avocado
is consumed around
the world.

Globally, 9.5 billion litres of water are used daily to produce avocado, which is the equivalent of 3,800 Olympic pools.

Top 10 Avocado Producers

1. Mexico
2. Dominican Republic
3. Peru
4. Indonesia
5. Columbia
6. Kenya
7. United States of America
8. Rwanda
9. Chile
10. Brazil

All avocados
are picked by hand.

A professional avocado
picker can pluck about
3,600 avocados a
day using a specially
equipped pole.

Avocados are graded
1 to 3 when picked, from
the visually pleasing
to runts of the harvest,
which go into animal
feed. You'll always be
buying a number 1 from
the supermarket.

Avocado is 73% water.

Avocados are
climacteric, meaning
they mature on the tree
but ripen off it.

The world record for the heaviest avocado is held by the Pokini family in Kahului, Hawaii, USA, set on 14 December 2018. Their avocado weighed in at an avo-mazing 2.55 kg.

Google "avocado recipe" and you'll get 221 million results. Fancy some guacamole?

You've got 44,900,000 to choose from.

Avo Joke #1

What is a priest's favourite food?

Holy guacamole!

The first known written account of the avocado as we know it was in 1519 by Martín Fernández de Enciso:

"... here are groves of many different sorts of edible fruits, among others is one which looks like an orange, and when it is ready for eating it turns yellowish; that which it contains is like butter and is of marvellous flavour, so good and pleasing to the palate that it is a marvellous thing."

Hans Sloane (of Sloane Square fame) is the person we have to thank for the English word avocado.

He coined the term when cataloguing plants on a trip to Jamaica in 1696.

#avocado

has been used over
13 million times on
Instagram.

A celebrity in the avocado world, the origins of the Hass avocado are un-guaca-believable. On a whim, Rudolf Hass, like a modern-day Jack and the Beanstalk, went to his local nursery to purchase some magical avocado seeds, having seen an article claiming they grew like money on trees.

All attempts failed. Nothing he did worked. So, with an axe in hand, he decided to just cull his failure and give up.

Thankfully, the avocado gods
were present and he was
stopped. The avocados that
eventually grew were different
from what they already knew, in
an avo-lutely brilliant way.
It was the best avocado anyone
had ever tasted!

Fast-forward to 1935 and the
popularity of this new avocado
surpassed all expectations,
and Hass patented his "Hass"
avocado tree.

The single Hass avocado
mother tree that Hass planted
survived until 2002, and it
is estimated that there are
5 million Hass avocado trees
in California and 10 million
worldwide – all descendants of
that one tree at 430 West Road,
La Habra Heights, California.

The word "guacamole" is a derivation of the Aztec word *ahuacamolli*, which translates loosely as "avocado soup" or "avocado sauce".

Avo Joke #2

What did the tortilla chip say to the guacamole?

"You are all I avo wanted."

As the first to start cultivating the avocado, it's no surprise that the Aztecs were the first to mash the fruit with tomatoes and chillies to make guacamole.

"Ahuaca-mulli", which literally translates as "avocado sauce" or "concoction", was so loved by the 16th-century Spanish explorers that they bought the recipe back to Spain, where it was altered over the centuries to become the guacamole we now know.

Top 5 Avocado Accompaniments

Vegetables: Peppers, carrots and celery are great low-calorie choices to pair with guacamole.

Bacon: Strips of well-fried streaky bacon add a satisfying crunch.

Potato wedges: Hot, paprika-sprinkled potato wedges are the perfect accompaniment to cool, fresh guacamole.

Shrimp: Buttery, warm shrimp coated in creole spices bring to life the guacamole, New Orleans style.

Homemade tortilla chips: If you can't beat them, join them. Slice fresh corn tortillas into wedges, bake in the oven in a single layer for 6 minutes, flip and bake again for another 6 minutes. Sprinkle with salt when they are fresh out of the oven.

Santa Barbara County, USA, holds the California Avocado Festival on the first week of October, having done so since 1986.

National Avocado Day is celebrated on 31 July.

National Guacamole Day is celebrated on 16 September.

Dr Jean's Banana Dance (aka The Guacamole Song) has been viewed over 37 million times on her YouTube channel.

You have to see it to believe it!

As niches go, American kindie rock bands are a good one. Add award-winning and you get Rolie Polie Guacamole, the Brooklyn-based parentally approved rock band.

Two decades on since they formed, they are still churning out the hits, including the incredibly catchy "Avocado" ("Aquacate" for their Spanish-speaking fans).

Celebrity fans of the avocado include Tom Selleck and Jason Mraz, who both own their own avocado farms.

Want to ditch those plastic straws? Pick up one made from an avocado seed instead.

Compared to a plastic straw, which can take 100 years to degrade, the avo straw does it in just 240 days.

CHAPTER
TWO

Smashing boundaries

The avocado is a superfood – and for good reason. From lowering your cholesterol to moisturising your hair, there are lots of different ways to make the most of this little green goddess. "Half an avocado a day keeps the doctor away" – or so it should go.

Avocados hold the world record for the highest calorific value of 38 fruits commonly eaten raw.

Just half an avocado counts as one of your five a day.

Avocados can act as a
"nutrient booster" by
enabling the body to
absorb more fat-soluble
nutrients, such as
vitamins A, D, E and K,
in foods that are eaten
with the fruit.

Avocados contain more potassium than bananas, which helps your muscles work, including those that control your heartbeat and breathing.

Trying to regulate
your blood pressure?
Avocados may do
wonders for keeping
your levels in check
because of their high
potassium and low
sodium content.

Avocados can help keep your eyes healthy. They are high in antioxidants including the carotenoids lutein and zeaxanthin, which are incredibly important for eye health.

They have even been linked to reducing the risk of cataracts and macular degeneration.

Rich in monounsaturated fat, avocados can not only help reduce your cholesterol, but also lower your risk of stroke and heart disease.

A 2012 Harvard study shows how eating avocado and monounsaturated fats as a part of a fertility diet may impact the success of IVF treatments.

Just 100g of avocado a day
contains 27% of our daily
recommended fibre and there
is strong evidence that
eating plenty of fibre can lower
your risk of heart disease,
stroke, type 2 diabetes and
bowel cancer.

Another bonus is that fibre
also makes us feel fuller,
can help digestion and
prevent blockages.

Avocados contain beta-sitosterol, a kind of plant sterol, which may help relieve symptoms of an enlarged prostate.

Half of an avocado
provides approximately
25% of the daily
recommended intake
of vitamin K, which is
essential for bone growth.

Avocados can help boost brain power.

All the nutrients in avocado can help increase your energy levels, fight fatigue and put you in a good mood.

Enjoyed the sunshine
a little too much?

Slather yourself in
avocado to help treat
sunburn.

Avocados have anti-inflammatory properties which can help to relieve arthritis pain.

They're also a source of omega-3 fatty acids, which help lubricate joints and further relieve joint pains.

Avocados can help you look younger!

They are a rich source of vitamin E, a powerful antioxidant that may be effective at reducing UV damage in skin.

The vitamin C in avocados may help reduce skin inflammation, accelerate wound healing and soothe dry skin.

If you're expecting a baby,
then eating avocado is a
good thing.

It contains folate, a B-vitamin
that is needed to make red
and white blood cells in
the bone marrow, convert
carbohydrates into energy, and
produce DNA and RNA.

Feeding your little one avocado as one of their first foods is an excellent idea.

Not only is the creamy texture and mild flavour perfect for their developing palates, but it is perfectly suited to their growing development.
The "Avocado Baby" had the right idea!

One downside to avocados: if you have a latex allergy, you may want to give the avocado toast a miss.

Avocado contains some of the same allergens found in latex, so they have the potential to trigger the same allergic reaction.

CHAPTER
THREE

Ripe enough for you?

Brown paper bag? Banana? Or the oven? We've all been there at some point: standing in the supermarket looking around to see if we're going to be caught squeezing every "perfectly ripe" avocado. Well, fear no more. Here are some top tips for you to pick through to ensure that your avocado is perfectly ripe before you cut into it, as well as some other useful tips to ensure you don't end up in the pits.

According to Avocados Australia, the average avocado is touched by four would-be shoppers before it's bought.

The three stages of avocado ripeness by colour:

Bright green: underripe

Purplish black: ripe

Black: overripe

Checking under the stem of the avocado is another way to test its ripeness:

"If under the nubby stem is green, the avo is ready to be seen. If it's brown, put it down."

While not available to us mere mortals, farms in Australia have started using infrared technology to check for internal bruising in avocados before shipping them.

Need to ripen an avocado in a rush?

Pop the avocado in a paper bag with a banana and it should be ripe in a day or two. The gas ethene is responsible for this trick.

Alternatively, you can bury the avocado in a bowl of rice, or simply sit your avocado on a sunny windowsill and the warmth of the sunlight will also speed up the ripening process.

To fridge or not to fridge?

This one depends on whether your avocado is already ripe and when you want to it eat.

Ripe avocado and ready
to eat it soon?

Fridge it.

Unripe avocado and
ready to eat it soon?

Leave it out.

You can freeze an avocado if you need to, but it's best to peel, deseed and chop the avocado before popping it into a freezer-safe container.

“

People who put
avocados in the fridge
are basically saying,
'I want to eventually
experience something
less amazing.'

"

Gregor Collins, author of *The Accidental Caregiver*

Oxygen is the enemy that turns your green avocado flesh brown in a process called enzymatic browning. Cover the green flesh of an avocado in lemon juice and wrap in cling film to stop it turning brown. It should be fine for a day or two.

If you don't have any lemons on hand, you can use lime juice, olive oil or even submerge the avocado in water to prevent that nasty browning on a cut avocado.

In 2020, avocados sprayed with a tasteless, edible plant-based coating went on sale in Europe. The treated avocados stay ripe for twice as long as usual, reducing both food and plastic packaging waste.

> **"**
> You'd better let
> somebody eat you,
> Let somebody eat you.
> Ya better let
> somebody eat you,
> Before it's too late.
> **"**

Weird Al Yankovic, "Avocado"

Overripe avocados?

It's not a disaster. They can be mashed and added to scrambled eggs for a perfect brunch alternative.

Adding equal amounts of overripe mashed avocados to plain organic yogurt, with a pinch of cumin, a pinch of chilli powder and salt to taste, makes a deliciously creamy salad dressing.

Another way to use up overripe avocados is to make a creamy pasta sauce.

Simply sauté some onions and garlic with your choice of spices, then stir in some chopped olives, fresh diced tomatoes, and your overripe avocado.

Simmer until the flavours meld and the sauce thickens, then pour over pasta.

"

Avocados, it's a
food that ain't worth
injuring yourself for. If
it's a hassle to get into,
leave it to the experts.

"

Karl Pilkington

Two words: Avocado Hand.

It might seem like a joke, but avocado hand is actually a thing. And very painful. The term was coined when the rise in the avocado's popularity hit an all-time high – as did people slicing their hands open trying to hack out the seed. It's not just us mortals that have yet to master the correct way to remove the seed. In 2012, Meryl Streep confirmed that avocado hand really is the . . . pits.

How to Properly Cut an Avocado

Ready, pitmister? Here we go.

1. Find a perfectly ripe avocado.

2. Cut the avocado in half using your best sharp knife, pushing the knife into the avocado until you feel the seed (pit).

3. Now rotate the knife around the avocado until you meet where you started. Mind those fingers!

4. Remove the knife and place safely somewhere nearby.

5. Gently twist both sides of the avocado away from each other and pull apart.

Congratulations! But here comes the danger. First, make sure you've got a suitable ugly tea towel somewhere ... just in case, you know, you need to stem some bleeding.

6. Take your best sharp knife and whack it into the seed. You're aiming to get the middle of the knife in the middle of the avocado. Don't stab it. That tea towel will be your friend far sooner that way.

7. Once the knife is wedged in the seed, you're halfway there. Step back and congratulate yourself for getting this far without injury. You're doing a lot better than some.

8. Now, twist the knife embedded in the seed and pull away.

9. Ta da! One seed stuck on one really sharp knife. This is not the moment to lose concentration. You may be giddy with your success, but you're not out of the woods yet.

10. Do not - we repeat - DO NOT grab the seed with your hand and try to prise it off your best sharp knife. Tempting as that might be, it's going to end in tears that way. Avocado seeds are slippery buggers, so we recommend using a bowl or the side of the bin to ping the avocado seed off the knife. Trust us, it works a treat.

The Avocado Fan
Level: Beginner

1. Once you've removed the seed from your avocado, gently remove as much of the flesh in one piece. The best way to do this is to scoop around and under the flesh with a spoon.

2. Now that you have your naked avocado half, lie it seed side down and take your best sharp knife. As thinly as possible, slice the avocado lengthways.

3. With a firm touch, gently push the avocado sideways. *Avo-cadabra* – one fanned avocado!

The Shaved Avocado
Level: Beginner

1. For this one, we'd recommended starting with a slightly underripe avocado.

2. Once you've removed the seed from your avocado, gently remove as much of the flesh in one piece.

3. Now use a vegetable peeler to gently scrape the flesh of the avocado, making long strokes lengthways.

The Avocado Rose
Level: Expert

1. Follow the instructions for The Avocado Fan (*see page 108*), but rather than slicing it lengthways, this time slice it sideways. (Top tip: discard about half an inch of the tip end as it makes it easier to form the flower.)

2. Once you've have sliced the whole half of the avocado, with a firm touch start pushing the avocado into a line about an inch wide. You're aiming to fan it out into a conga dancing line of avocado slices.

3. Now start at the top of the avocado where you began cutting and start to roll it into the centre, creating a spiral shape.

4. Move gently as you work your way along the avocado, winding it up as you go.

5. Once all the avocado is wound around itself, gently open the slices or petals of avocado and – voila! – you have an avo-lutely beautiful rose.

If avocado art isn't your thing, then you can always use an egg slicer on a peeled and deseeded avocado to get those perfect slices.

Not washing your avocado before cutting into it? Current recommendations are that you should wash an avocado before you dig in. Literally.

While the skin protects the flesh, cutting into an unwashed avocado can push bacteria living on the skin into the flesh.

CHAPTER
FOUR

"Hold my avocado"

A 21st-century staple in every household, it's hard to fathom a time when an avocado wasn't found happily snuggled up to your milk and eggs in your shopping basket. But how did the avocado end up being the emerald green superfood of choice when it was barely known 100 years ago? And how did it manage to sneak into every corner shop, household and brunch menu across the land?

Scientists have unearthed evidence from a cave in Mexico's Coxcatlan which reveals that avocados were used as far back as 10,000 BCE.

Avocado tree cultivation started in Central America and South America somewhere around 5,000 BCE.

While the avocado has been planted in the United States since the 1830s, they were just considered ornamental plants.

By the 1900s, luxury hotels in Los Angeles and San Francisco were selling the fruits at $1 a go (equivalent to $24 or £18 in today's money), earning them the nickname "Green Gold".

Before 1915, the avocado
was still referred to as
"ahuacate" in California,
a throwback from Martín
Fernández de Enciso
and the less attractive
"alligator pear" in Florida.

It wasn't until May 1915, the birth of the California Avocado Association, that the "ahuacate" or "alligator pear" became the avocado.

Avo Joke #3

What's an avocado's
favourite music?
Guac 'n' Roll

Other terms still used
for avocado are "alligator
pear", "butter pear",
"vegetable butter" and
"midshipman's butter".

The common name for the avocado in Chinese is 牛油果 (niúyóuguǒ), which literally means "butterfruit" or "cow oil fruit".

Building on the growing popularity and a moment of pure genius in 1926, the California Avocado Society decided to promote the avocado as the "aristocrat of salad fruits".

Adverts taken out in *Vogue* and the *New Yorker* promoted eating the fruit stuffed into lobster and slicing it with grapefruit into a salad.

In countries where Spanish
is the official language, there are
many different names for an
avocado.

Aguacata
is the ancient term still used.

Aguacate
is used in Spain, El Salvador
and Colombia.

Aguaco
is another common term.

Ahuaca
is still used but is less popular.

Cura

is the way Venezuelans used to refer this popular superfood.

Pagua

is the most popular word for avocado in Cuba.

Palta

is one of the most common ways to say avocado in Spanish, used in Chile, Peru, Uruguay, Bolivia and Argentina.

Persea

can be used to talk about both the tree and its fruit.

It wasn't until the 1950s
and mass production began
stateside that the price of an
avocado dropped from $1
to the more reasonable cost of
25 cents.

Exporting the fruit then
became a much richer
possibility and avocados finally
reached the shores of Britain.

Since 1914, the United States had banned Mexican avocados because of fears of an insect infestation and cheaper competition.

The year 1994, however, was a game changer – Mexico, Canada and the United States enacted the North American Free Trade Agreement, with the US soon lifting its ban, marking the avocado explosion that followed.

In 1962, Sainsbury's introduced the British public to the avocado, swiftly followed by Marks and Spencer's in 1968. Marketing them as avocado pears turned out to be a mistake, however.

Angry letters swiftly arrived from those who had stewed them and served them with custard. As a result, the company had to produce a recipe leaflet explaining to customers what to do with the "new" fruit.

Marks and Spencer's caused further outrage when they started selling pre-sliced avocados, with many commenting that it was a shame that avocados didn't come in their own natural packaging already!

In 2018, the '70s avocado bathroom suite topped a survey as the "most regrettable interior trend".

The avocado was an unlikely enemy of the low-fat craze of the 1980s.

Falling out of favour as fast as you can say Jane Fonda, the avocado was suddenly seen as a ticking time bomb of fat.

America introduced Mr Ripe Guy to the masses in 1990s in an attempt to bolster its popularity.

What better way to promote the avocado than dressing a man in a giant avocado costume, travelling around in his avocado-coloured car giving out free avocados? Sniggering aside, it worked.

"Guacamole Bowl" was America's other answer to promoting the benefits of the avocado.

It was simple: take the biggest sporting event in the American calendar: the Super Bowl. Send out guacamole samples to the general public, and persuade a raft of NFL celebrities to share their guacamole recipes. The rest, as they say, is history.

In the US, 20% of all avocado sales take place on Super Bowl Sunday, and it's estimated that, on average, 53.5 million lbs (24 million kg) are eaten on this day alone.

"Avocados from Mexico"
was the first brand in the
agricultural sector to pay
for a television commercial
during the Super Bowl.

There's no arguing that the avocado reached its peak in 2017, when it became the symbol of every millennial's failure to climb the housing ladder.

When Australian real estate mogul Tim Gurner advised millennials that they could solve all their housing woes by forgoing their expensive avocado on toast and coffee rituals and put the money towards a deposit instead, it caused an uproar.

While the advice might have been given in good faith, most argued that they weren't spending their money on avocado toast instead of buying houses; they were spending the money because there was little chance of managing to get a deposit large enough to afford a house.

One millennial argued that even if they quit their habit, it would take them 175 years to save up enough.

When the trend for proposing with a ring hidden inside an avocado hit "mainstream" in 2018, Asda decided to give them a helping hand by printing "Perfect for a proposal" on the best specimens.

Avocados may be the best source of food we have when we get to Mars.

Scientists at Australia's University of Queensland cryopreserved the shoots of avocado plants to test whether they could be sent to Mars as a food source.

And it worked. After thawing them out, two months later the shoots started growing leaves again.

The makers of Monopoly hit the pits in 2018 when they released a "Cheaters Edition" of the game, complete with a "Someone has stolen your avocado from the farmers market".

Sushi was introduced to America by Ichiro Mashita in Los Angeles in the late '60s.

After substituting avocado for tuna, he is credited with creating the "California Roll".

In 2019, an Israeli woman was hospitalised after mistaking wasabi for avocado. She was diagnosed with takotsubo cardiomyopathy, more commonly known as broken heart syndrome.

The condition is often triggered by extreme emotional or physical stress, hence the name.

Shockingly, in the UK's top 10 most popular foods on Instagram in 2018, the **avocado** (with 271,789 posts) was beaten to the top spot by **curry** (551,701 posts). Nevertheless, it comfortably vanquished some truly classic British favourites: **fish and chips** (63,856), **Yorkshire pudding** (51,55), **cream tea** (45,189), **sausage roll** (29,113), **trifle** (11,359), **chip butty** (9,121), **Cornish pasty** (6,393) and **beef wellington** (2,432).

Brooklyn, New York,
is home to Avocaderia,
the world's first
avocado bar.

If you're looking for just avocados, then the mono-product restaurant chain The Avocado Show is your thing. They have locations in London, Amsterdam, Madrid and Brussels.

Avocados in New Zealand hit an all-time high when they were selling at $10 NZ a piece (£5) in early 2019.

Lockdown in 2020 saw the price drop almost 62%, however, as the country experienced a glut when restaurants and cafes were forced to shut.

In 2019, some taco stands in Mexico were substituting "calabacitas" – a bright green Mexican squash – for avocados in their guacamole. The reason? Avocado prices had soared and no one noticed the difference!

When many millennials failed to get their hands on a discount railcard in 2018, Virgin Trains came to the rescue by simply asking them to present an avocado in place of the railcard when booking their ticket.

Sadly, this offer was only valid for a week.

Camilo Briceño, a Chilean avocado dealer who goes by the name *"el weon de las paltas"* (the avocado guy), bought a £300 mobile phone in exchange for 58 kg of avocados.

How did he know it was 58 kg? Because the retailer had listed the recommended retail costs and its equivalent value in avocados.

CHAPTER
FIVE

Pass me
the avocado

There are other ways to eat an
avocado other than layering it onto
toast in an Instagram-worthy fashion.

Shocking, we know.

Avocado Butter

1 avocado
¼ cup (60g) soft butter
½ lime

Spread it on toast, melt it into sweet potatoes, smother it over fresh corn . . . however you use it, avocado butter will be your new go-to.

Simply place the flesh of the avocado, the butter, the juice of half a lime and a little salt in a food processor and mix until smooth and well combined. Serve immediately, or wrap in plastic and refrigerate until firm for sliceable butter.

If you're feeling a little lazy,
instead of spreading a
layer of mayonnaise on a bun,
just add a few slices
of avocado.

You achieve the same
creaminess in a lighter,
vegan way.

Baked Avocados

1 avocado
2 eggs
Pinch of chives

For a simple, delicious and avo-mazing brunch option, place your avocado halves on a baking tray and scoop out a little of the flesh to create wells.

Crack an egg into each of the wells, season and pop into a preheated oven (220°C/430°F) for 15 minutes or until the eggs are cooked. Sprinkle with chives and enjoy!

Avocado Tea

1 avocado seed
2 cups (475ml) hot water

Looking for an alternative to mint tea?
Avocado tea might be the one for you. It can
help with digestion, is low in calories and has
anti-inflammatory properties.

To make your own, take the seed of one avocado
and boil it for 5 minutes. The seed will have now
softened enough for it to be cut into pieces (you
can also grate it or use a coffee grinder).

Drop the cut pieces into a cafetière or teapot,
add the hot water and let it steep for 7–8
minutes. Strain the tea if using a teapot before
enjoying, and add honey or another
sweetener for a stronger flavour.

Avocado and Eggs on Toast Avolatte

1 avocado
Pinch garlic powder/1 garlic clove
Pinch chili flakes
½ lime
Small bunch coriander (optional)

Why mess with perfection? There's a good reason this dish is on any self-respecting brunch menu: the holy trinity of eggs, avocado and bread combines to make something greater than its parts.

Simply smash the avocado flesh in a bowl with the garlic powder (or grated fresh garlic), chili flakes, a pinch of salt, a grind of black pepper, a squeeze of lime juice and a dash of extra virgin olive oil. You can add finely chopped coriander too if you fancy. Generously dollop onto toasted sourdough and top with a fried or poached egg. A true classic.

Breakfast Tacos

5 oz (150g) spinach
3 eggs
4 tortillas
½ lime (optional)
Avocado salsa verde

Ditch your cereal or toast for this Mexican-inspired breakfast taco.

In a lightly oiled pan, sauté the spinach until wilted, then set aside. Wipe out your pan, or grab a clean one, melt a knob of butter and scramble the eggs until just set. Warm each tortilla for a few seconds in a hot dry pan then top with eggs, spinach and avocado salsa verde (*see page 160*) or a simple avocado salsa (*see page 161*).

Pimp up your taco by adding fried mushrooms, bacon, warm black beans or refried beans. Add a squeeze of lime before eating for a fresh hit.

Avocado Salsa Verde

2 cloves garlic
1 avocado
2 handfuls parsley
1 handful basil
Small handful capers
3 tbsp red wine vinegar
1 tbsp Dijon mustard

A twist on the classic, this turns the herby Mexican sauce into something creamier and somehow even more delicious.

Blitz the garlic and avocado flesh in a blender until smooth. Finely chop the parsley, basil and capers; mix with the blended avocado and garlic. Add the red wine vinegar, a glug of extra virgin olive oil and the Dijon mustard. Add chopped jalapeno for some heat, and a squeeze of lime will help keep it fresh.

Simple Avocado Salsa

½ red onion
3 tomatoes
2 avocados
Small red chili
Small bunch coriander
½ lime

Sometimes simple is best – this salsa is a breeze to make and can be added to a near-endless list of dishes.

Finely chop the red onion, tomatoes, avocados, red chili and a small bunch of coriander, including the stalks. Add to a large bowl with a glug of olive oil, a sprinkle of salt and a healthy squeeze of lime juice, then toss to combine. To boost the lime, add the zest of the lime, or up the heat with extra chili.

For an unusual and fruity twist, add a little chopped mango.

Avocado Smoothie

½ avocado
1 frozen banana
1 cup (250ml) milk of your choice
1 tsp vanilla extract
1 tbsp sweetener (agave, maple syrup
or similar)

Does the idea of spinach or kale in your morning smoothie put you off? Or are you looking to mix up your breakfast choices?

This smoothie is both super tasty and a great way to get your green goodness in for the day. Simply blend together the avocado flesh, frozen banana, milk, vanilla extract and a squeeze of sweetener (try agave or maple syrup). Add a little more milk if it comes out too thick.

Experiment with adding frozen pineapple, blueberries or other fruit, or add a scoop of protein powder if that's your thing.

Classic Guacamole

2 avocados
½ red onion
1 small red chili
1 large ripe tomato
Handful of coriander
½ lime

Think avocado and you probably think guacamole.

Smash the avocados in a bowl, leaving it a little chunky for texture. Finely chop the red onion, red chili and ripe tomato and add to the bowl. Add salt, pepper, chopped coriander and a good squeeze of lime juice, then mix well.

Eat quickly while it's fresh - grab those tortilla chips and get stuck in.

Avocado, Halloumi and Squash Salad

1 cup (150g) butternut squash
2 tsp paprika
100g quinoa
200ml cold water
100g halloumi
1 avocado
100ml olive oil
2 tbsp honey
1 lemon
100g spinach leaves

This salad is great eaten fresh or works well as a lunch the next day. The mix of textures and sweet/salty combination means this is sure to become a favourite.

First, cube the butternut squash, drizzle over some oil and smoked paprika and roast until soft and slightly charred. Meanwhile, cover the quinoa with the cold water and bring to a boil. Reduce the heat and simmer for 10-15 minutes until the water has been absorbed; rest for 5 minutes then fluff with a fork. Fry slices of halloumi for a few minutes each side until golden brown.

Cube the flesh of the ripe avocado. Mix the olive oil, a squeeze of honey and the juice of the lemon together, then set aside. Pile spinach leaves or rocket, the quinoa, butternut squash and halloumi onto plates and drizzle over the dressing. Try topping with pomegranate seeds, walnuts, toasted pine nuts or pumpkin seeds.

Funky Guacamoles

A classic guacamole is always a winner. But what if you want to mix it up? Here are a few more unusual ideas.

Bacon guac: Cook a couple of slices of bacon really well and crumble on top of the guac; this adds a whole new salty, crunchy, meaty twist.

Fruity guac: Finely chop some mango and scatter with pomegranate seeds onto the guac; it's fun, fruity and fresh.

Charred corn guac: Fire up a BBQ, or a hot griddle pan, and char a couple of corn on the cob. Slice the corn from the cob and top the guac; it's a sweet yet smoky change.

Tahini and feta guac: Everything's better with cheese, so crumble some feta over your guac and drizzle over a spoonful of tahini.

Avocado Club Sandwich

Just when you think something can't be improved, along comes avocado to prove you wrong. Turns out all the iconic club sandwich needed was an extra creamy green layer to really take it to the next level.

Assemble your normal club sandwich – with streaky bacon, chicken or turkey slices, mayonnaise, tomato, lettuce and lightly toasted bread – but add that special ingredient. It doesn't matter whether you slice, smash or smear the avo, just make sure it's in there.

Avocado Pasta

1½ cups (180g) dried pasta
1 avocado
2 handfuls spinach leaves
1 tbsp olive oil
1 clove garlic
Small handful basil leaves
1 tsp chili flakes
1 lemon

This is a beautifully creamy and fresh pasta dish that's secretly vegan.

Cook the pasta to the packet instructions, adding a pinch of salt to the water. Blitz the flesh of the avocado, the spinach leaves, olive oil, garlic clove, basil leaves, a pinch of chili flakes and the juice and zest of the lemon. Add a splash more oil to loosen if needed. Drain the pasta but retain some water, then mix the pasta with the blitzed avocado and a splash of the pasta water. Mix so the pasta is coated.

Finish with black pepper and fresh basil leaves.

Avocado Chocolate Mousse

⅓ cup (75g) dark chocolate (plus extra
for topping)
4 tbsp maple syrup (or agave)
2 tsp vanilla extract
¼ tsp salt
2½ tbsp cocoa powder
5 tbsp milk of your choice (coconut works well)
2 avocados

Like chocolate and chili, chocolate and avocado
sounds wrong until you try it . . . and you realize
it's so right. This mousse is thick, smooth and
super chocolatey.

Melt the dark chocolate in a bain-marie, stirring
in the maple syrup (or agave), vanilla extract,
salt, cocoa powder and milk. Pour into a blender
with the flesh of the avocados and blend until
smooth. Split between 6 glasses and chill for a
few hours. Grate some extra chocolate on top, or
top with fresh strawberries or raspberries. Tuck
in and enjoy.

Gargling with cold avocado tea is also a natural way to deal with toothache.

Jus Alpukat (Iced Avocado)

1 avocado
1 cup (250ml) coffee
½ cup (25ml) sweetened condensed milk
2 cups ice
2 tsp vanilla extract

If you're looking for something with a little caffeine hit, then maybe the Indonesian Jus Alpukat is for you.

This creamy, frappe-like drink combines avocados, coffee and condensed milk into a smashing drink that's perfect for a hot day. Just add the flesh of the avocado, the coffee, condensed milk and vanilla extract to a blender. Blend until smooth, then pour and enjoy.

You can top it with chocolate syrup or even add a shot of vodka or chocolate liqueur to spice things up a bit.

Ever heard of an **avolatte**?

No, it's not just another terrible pun. In fact, as the name suggests, it is a latte served in the scooped-out shell of an avocado.

Legend has it that it started off as a joke by a Melbourne coffee house, but it went viral in 2017 and people actually bought them.

Dry and grate the seed of an avocado to make a traditional North Mexican enchilada sauce that tastes really authentic.

Leave a clean avocado in a cool, dry place for 5-7 days, then grate it into small bits (a food processor really helps). Add this to your sauce before baking. About 1½ teaspoons should do the trick - any more, and the dish may end up tasting too bitter!

Avo Joke #4

What do you call two male avocados who hang out and drink together?

Avocabros

Did you know you can pickle avocados?

It might sound odd, but pickling is a fantastic way to preserve ripe and ready avocados.

Simply combine vinegar, water, sugar and salt with herbs of your choice in a jar, cover tightly and leave for a few hours in the fridge.

Grilled avocado

BBQs aren't just for sausages and hamburgers. Fancy adding a bit of greenery to yours?

Just cut an avocado in half, remove the seed and brush with olive oil. Place them seed-side down on the grill and cook for 5 minutes.

Avocados add moisture
to cakes without the
need for butter, creating
a beautiful fudge-like
decadence!

Avocado Ice Cream

3 avocados
400ml sweetened condensed milk
1 lime
1 cup (240ml) cream
½ cup (120ml) milk

Add the avocado flesh, condensed milk,
lime juice, cream and milk to a blender and
puree until smooth. (Add more cream if the
mixtures feels very thick and heavy.)

Transfer the mixture to a freezer-safe container
and chill for four hours, then process the
mixture in an ice cream machine for about
20 minutes or until it sets.

Avocado Popsicles

2 avocados
1 cup (240ml) coconut milk
2 tbsp honey
½ lime

Pastel-green popsicles with healthy kick.

Add the avocado flesh, coconut milk, honey and lime juice to a blender and puree until smooth. Pour into moulds and freeze for at least 2 hours.

Avocado Popcorn

While it might sound avo-solutely wrong, just try it and see.

If you're a fan of buttered popcorn, this might just be your next favourite movie-night treat. Just add diced avocado, olive oil and salt (chilli lime too, if you can find it) to plain popcorn.

Avocado Pesto

1 avocado
4 cups (80g) basil
½ cup (50g) pine nuts
½ cup (50g) parmesan
⅔ cup olive oil
2 cloves garlic

We all know about basil pesto and have probably had a go at making it at home ourselves. So why not go one step further and try making avocado pesto?

Just add diced avocado flesh to the usual suspects of basil, pine nuts, garlic, parmesan and olive oil. Blend and enjoy. Drop the parmesan to make it vegan . . . either way, it's smashing!

CHAPTER
SIX

Hass enough already?

They might be the green goddess, but you can have too much of a good, even healthy, thing. While we are strong believers in the health benefits of eating an avocado a day, if you've reached the pit of your avocado enthusiasm, then here are some great things to do with them that don't involve actually eating them.

Avocado facemask

Blend together half a ripe avocado, 1 egg, 1 tbsp Greek yogurt and 1 tsp baking soda. Apply to your face immediately.

Sit back and relax until you feel it starting to tighten. Rinse with warm water and admire beautiful, moisturised skin.

Avocado hair mask

Blend half a ripe banana with
1 ripe avocado. Apply to damp
hair and let the mixture work
its magic for 30 minutes.

You can add 2 tsp of honey
for an additional moisture hit
or 1 tsp of olive oil and 1 tsp of
coconut oil for extra shine.

Make your own avocado oil

If you have an orange press this one is simple – just stack avocado skins on top of each other, give them a good press and – avo-cadabra – your very own virgin avocado oil!

Just when you thought there wasn't much more you could do with an avocado – have you tried using the leaves? Dried avocado leaves can be ground down and used to flavour guacamole.

Placed under roasting meats or fish is also a fabulous way to add flavour to a dish. They have a subtle anise aroma and are a popular herb throughout central and southern Mexico.

Fresh avocado leaves can be used as they are in a salad or mashed to make a marinade or popped into the toaster as a tasty snack.

Make your own avocado dye

And no, it's not green. It's PINK!

1. Put cut skins and stones into a pan suitable to be heated on the hob.

2. Add tap water and bring to a simmer for 1 hour. You should get a pale pink colour which may turn a reddish brown.

3. Add the cloths to be dyed and simmer for another hour.

4. Leave overnight.

5. In the morning, wash the fabrics and you should have some beautiful, naturally dyed pale pink cloth.

Make indelible ink

1. Put the avocado seed in a heavy-duty plastic bag and crush it using something like a hammer or a brick.

2. The milky liquid that comes out will turn red or black when exposed to the air. Dip a calligraphy pen or a thin paintbrush into this liquid and use it to write or paint on a sheet of paper.

How to grow your own avocado tree with just a glass, water and some toothpicks

1. Carefully remove your avocado stone, avoiding cutting or breaking it.

2. Give it a wash and let it dry a bit.

3. Insert three toothpicks halfway up the stone.

4. Now, suspend the stone, broadside down in a glass of water, ensuring the bottom third of the stone is covered.

5. Leave in a warm, sunny spot out of direct sunlight, making sure you change the water regularly.

6. Between 2 and 6 weeks, you should start to see roots at the bottom and a sprout appear at the top. If not, don't despair – it's time to try again!

7. When you have a sprout that is about 6 inches (15 cm) tall, cut back to about half the height to encourage further root growth.

8. Once your plant has grown again to about 6 inches, it's time to repot in a 10-inch pot.

9. Congratulations! You have your own avocado tree.

It's worth noting that it can take anywhere between 5 and 13 years for an avocado tree to grow any fruit, and those kept indoors don't tend to, but it will still look beautiful!

How to grow your own avocado tree: Part 2

(the one with less toothpick faff)

1. Half-bury an avocado seed in a pot of gritty seed compost, pointy end up.

2. Give it a thorough water, cover the pot with a plastic bag to seal in the warmth and moisture, and then leave it alone.

3. Keep it in a warm place and you should begin to see signs of germination in 2 to 4 weeks.

4. Once the seed has sprouted, remove the plastic cover and keep it in a spot with bright, indirect light.

And bravo! One home-grown avocado plant!